ALLISON ADELLE HED
North Carolina, the Plains and C
waters, and factories, including w
Professor of Creative Writing (poetry/nonfiction) at the University of
California Riverside (narrative medicine in the UCR School of Medicine),
she has served as a Distinguished Visiting Writer for the University of
Hawai'i at Mānoa, founded and directs the Literary Sandhill Crane Retreat
at the migration epicenter, and the Along the Chaparral project. Recently
awarded the First Jade-Nurtured Sihui Female International Poetry Award
for Foreign Poet (2018), Hedge Coke has authored six books of poetry and a
memoir. Her recently edited anthologies include, *Effigies*, *Effigies II*, and *Sing:
Poetry from the Indigenous Americas*. *Effigies III* is her tenth edited volume.

DR. CRAIG SANTOS PEREZ is a native Chamorro from the Pacific Island
of Guåhan (Guam). He is the author of four collections of poetry, the co-editor
of three anthologies, and the co-founder of Ala Press (the only publisher in the
US dedicated to Pacific Islander poetry). For his writing and scholarship, he has
received a PEN Center USA/Poetry Society of America Literary Prize, American
Book Award, Lannan Foundation Literary Fellowship, Ford Foundation Fellowship,
and Hawai'i Literary Arts Council Award. Currently, he works as an Associate
Professor in the English Department at the University of Hawai'i, Mānoa, where he
received a Chancellors' Citation for Meritorious Teaching. His undergraduate and
graduate courses focus on environmental poetry, food writing, and Pacific literature.

From Kula, Maui, BRANDY NĀLANI MCDOUGALL, is of Kanaka 'Ōiwi
(Hawai'i, Maui, and Kaua'i lineages), Chinese and Scottish descent. She is the author
of a poetry collection, *The Salt-Wind, Ka Makani Pa'akai* (Kuleana 'Ōiwi Press
2008) and has edited three Pacific poetry anthologies. Her scholarly monograph
Finding Meaning: Kaona and Contemporary Hawai'ian Literature (University of
Arizona Press 2016) was awarded the 2017 Beatrice Medicine Award for Scholarship
in American Indian Studies. She is an Associate Professor specializing in Indigenous
Studies in the American Studies Department at the University of Hawai'i at Mānoa.

Effigies III

An Anthology of New Indigenous Writing Pacific Islands, 2018

Edited by
ALLISON ADELLE HEDGE COKE,
BRANDY NĀLANI MCDOUGALL
and CRAIG SANTOS PEREZ

SALT

CROMER

PUBLISHED BY SALT PUBLISHING 2019

2 4 6 8 10 9 7 5 3 1

First published in Great Britain in 2019 by
Salt Publishing Ltd
12 Norwich Road, Cromer, Norfolk NR27 0AX United Kingdom

www.saltpublishing.com

Salt Publishing Limited Reg. No. 5293401

A CIP catalogue record for this book is available from the British Library

ISBN 978 1 78463 183 3 (Paperback edition)

Typeset in Neacademia by Salt Publishing

Printed and bound in the United States of America by Lightning Source Inc

Contents

MAI KA PŌ MAI KA ʻOIAʻIʻO
Jamaica Heolimeleikalani Osorio

HĀNAU

KINO PĀPĀLUA

ŌLAʻI

HULIHIA

SERETAGI

PERMISSION TO MAKE DIGGING SOUNDS
No'u Revilla

EFFIGIES III

Acknowledgements

KISHA BORJA-QUICHOCHO-CALVO

'I could be Miss Guam Tourism' (Originally published in *Storyboard* 10.)

'Nåna' (Originally published in *Storyboard* 10 – *A Journal of Pacific Imagery* and *Micronesian Educator* – *A Journal of Research & Practice on Education in Guam and Micronesia*.)

'Para si Lina'la': Life Lesson #1' (Originally published in *Storyboard* 15 – *A Journal of Pacific Imagery*.)

'Para si Lina'la': Life Lesson #2' (Originally published in *Local Voices* – *An Anthology* [12th Festival of the Pacific Arts].)

'Sitting in History' (Originally published in *Aloha Shorts*, 2013.)

TAGI QOLOUVAKI

'Tell Me a Story (for uncle Talanoa)' (Originally in *Mauri Ola: Contemporary Polynesian Poems in English*. Eds. Albert Wendt, Reina Whaitiri and Robert Sullivan. Auckland: Auckland University Press. 2010.)

'For Nico' (Originally in *Mauri Ola: Contemporary Polynesian Poems in English*. Eds. Albert Wendt, Reina Whaitiri and Robert Sullivan. Auckland: Auckland University Press. 2010.)

'Masu' (Originally in *Ika* 2. Ed. Anne Kennedy. Auckland: Manikau Institute of Technology. 2014.)

'Suka' (Originally in *Hawai'i Review Editor's Blog*. "Community Poetry with Craig Santos Perez." Ed. No'u Revilla. Honolulu. 2013.)

'No-Name Poem' (Originally in *Diasporadic*. (Zine) Ed. Luisa Tora. Auckland. 2011 and VASU: Pacific Women of Power. Eds. Cresantia Frances Koya and Luisa Tora. Suva: Oceania Printers Ltd. 2008.)

l'olomaloha: fruit for aiko' (Originally in in *Banninur: A Basket of Food*. Eds. Kathy Jetnil-Kijiner and Katherine Higgins. Honolulu: black mail press and the Center for Pacific Island Studies, UHM. 2014.)

'Kokoda (for Tere)' (Originallu in *Banninur: A Basket of Food*. Eds. Kathy Jetnil-Kijiner and Katherine Higgins. Honolulu: black mail press and the Center for Pacific Island Studies, UHM. 2014.)

'Cawaki / sea urchin stories she sung me/for katalaine' (Originally in Introduction to Women's, Gender, and Sexuality Studies. Eds. Ayu Saraswati, Barbara Shaw, and Heather Rellihan. Oxford: Oxford University Press. 2017.)

NOʻU REVILLA

'Make Rice' (Originally published in *Say Throne* by Tinfish Press.)

'Getting Ready for Work' (Originally published in *Say Throne* by Tinfish Press.)

'Ceremony' (Originally published in *The Value of Hawaiʻi 2*.)

'Rope / Tongue' (Originally published in *Say Throne* by Tinfish Press.)

Editors' Notes

The Effigies series has woven a vibrant tapestry of Indigenous poets from Native North America and the Pacific. This anthology furthers this braiding with the work of four emerging islander women poets from Guam, Hawai'i, and Fiji. Despite their distant origins, all these writers explore culture, history, politics, genealogy, feminism, and the environment. They each have their own unique style, ranging from the lyric to the avant-garde. Overall, they represent the next resurgent wave of empowered and decolonial Pacific writers.

No'u Revilla (Kanaka 'Ōiwi), Jamaica Heolimeleikalani Osorio (Kanaka 'Ōiwi), Kisha Borja-Quichocho-Calvo (CHamoru), and Tagi Qolouvaki (Fijian, Tongan) take readers into the vast Pacific ocean to swim beyond the reef in high tide, out to where the water meets the sky, only to circle back to the islands to taste the tears and sweat in coconut and guava, the smell of frangipani on the wind. Amidst such beauty, these poets also carry us into darkness with tremendous power and vulnerability, laying bare the ravages of colonialism—the brutal occupation of country, the violence waged against Native women and girls, the erosion of language and ancestral memory, and the forced disconnections from land, ocean, and other healing lifeways. Effigies III features four debut books that fearlessly journey through these home-islands in ways that will transform and empower.

BRANDY NĀLANI MCDOUGALL
and DR. CRAIG SANTOS PEREZ

The power in these books is immense. These poets deliver Oceania diversity and centrality for the whole of the planet. Their meaningful poetics offer splendid horizons, reefs and riffs, locating us in the beauty and brutality of what is, has been, and will be. This synergistic compilation is truly of the best of new poetry and fishes each of us on a human level. In this tenuous moment of climate despair, the oceans are our redemption and deepest concern. These four poets deliver lifescale from upon and within the largest ocean and like the islands they come from ground us in the lineages and landscapes of home.

ALLISON ADELLE HEDGE COKE

DECOLONIZING MINDS WITH(IN)
BARBED-WIRE FENCELINES

Kisha Borja-Quichocho-Calvo

American He'e

American he'e.

The tentacles of this large creature are deadly
grabbing hold of the smallest peoples

choking us

so that we can't say anything

paralyzing us

so that action becomes an idea rather than a reality.

Until we come together
to bite between the eyes
of this monstrous creature,
it will continue to grab
each and every one of us,
disconnecting us from our homes,
feeding off our blood so it can

survive.

Our deaths allow for the he'e's survival.

But with our words of anger,
eyes of pain,
tongues of steel,
and the strongest of our arms

Kanaka Maoli

        Chamorus

Samoans

        Puerto Ricans

Okinawans

        Native Americans

can unify,
sharpen our teeth,
and bite the fuck out
of the
He'e.

Ocean Women's Mission

We are Ocean Women
      with a bloodline that runs into the
      far distance
      just like our Ocean
      into the horizon.
We have a mission Lina'lå'-hu:
      To protect our Ocean from harm
      so that every day, every time
      our People go to Her
They will know Her
      and will be able to call Her:
Past
Present
Future
Love
Mother

Home

Dear "Uncle Sam,"

Which star or stripe represents my island?

Why can't I find my island on your map?

Why can't Chamorus
vote for President as residents of Guåhan?

Why does our congresswoman just sit in your House,
only writing about what
she wish she could say?

Why does our flag
fly alongside the red flag with the big yellow arches,
below your red, white, and blue flag?

Why can't I speak my language, but I can speak yours?

"Uncle Sam":

If we're so "American"
like you say we are,
then which star or stripe
represents our island?

p.s. How are you my uncle?

What's your family name?

Dispensa Yu'

Guella yan Guello,
dispensa yu'.

Dispensa

yu'.

My tongue has been cut

off

replaced by a tongue
that belongs to someone else.

Guella yan Guello,
dispensa yu'.

My ears have been cut

off

replaced with ears
that belong to someone else.

Guella yan Guello,
dispensa yu'.

My eyes have been blinded by someone else.

Guela yan guello,
dispensa yu'.

Even though I can't speak to you
hear you

or see you

My heart—

It still feels you.

I could be Miss Guam Tourism

if I was 5'3"
and looked good in a bikini.

It doesn't matter
if I know Guåhan's culture and history,
how Chode Mart sells the crunchiest empañada on the island,
or that the best pickled mango can be found in the village of
    Talofo'fo'.
It doesn't matter
if I know that before one enters the jungle,
    she must say, "Guella yan Guello, kao siña humanao yu' para i
    tano' miyu"
    to show respect for her ancestors.
It doesn't matter if I know that "going around the island" with family
    means only going around the South.
And if I said that every Chamoru's childhood
    included going to Ipao Beach, capturing dukduk crabs in the
    sand,
    and playing with the thickest blackest balåti,
                             it still wouldn't matter.

I'm not 5'3".
My dågan can barely fit into a bikini.

M is for Micronesia(n)

"Micronesia" means
small
little
tiny
islands.
small
little
tiny
peoples—

No
job,
money,
education,
home.

We have no place to go,
        and people are complaining:

"Those Micronesians can't speak english properly."

"They look funny,
        with their tortoiseshell combs
        and their floral print skirts."

"They abuse the system."

"Micronesia" means
Chuuk
Pohnpei
Kosrae
Yap
Belau
Marshall Islands

Saipan
Guåhan
Luta
Tinian
Nauru
Kiribati
and so many other
small,
little,
tiny
islands.

But the people of these islands are
strong,
struggling in a system
that is working against them.
serving a country
that doesn't give a damn.

We often
lose a sister to diabetes,
a brother to suicide,
both to the armed forces.

We are barely surviving,
and this country

doesn't

give

a

damn.

It just complains

every

single

day—

We're too stupid,
too dirty,
too poor.

small,
little,
tiny.

Too

Micronesian.

My Culture is Alive

My culture is alive.
It is a living, breathing being
that walks and talks
dances and chants
carves and cooks
fishes, hunts, and farms

My culture listens.
Listens to the voices of our people chanting
calling on the past of our present
to unwrap what we have yet to know.
It listens to the movement of our women
swaying our hips and clapping our hands
and our men slapping their chests
and stomping their feet
to the beats of our culture's soul.

My culture listens.
Listens to the pounding hearts of my people
as we continue to engage in battles
which leave many of us baffled:
>   *Who* are we?
>   *What* are we?
>   *Where* are we?

We are left feeling disconnected and isolated.

Yet why
my culture asks
do we disconnect and isolate
when we should mate and proliferate
increase our numbers and spread.

My culture is not dead.

It is very much alive.
It is alive because I am standing.
It is alive because I am breathing.
It is alive because I exist.

And as long as I
and you
and you
and you
As long as WE
exist

Our culture will be kept alive.

Because it is what gives us life.

I hate when people say that
our culture is dead or dying

When they say that,
they either don't know any better
or they're not Chamoru.
I'd like to stick with the latter
because Chamorus
can't say their culture is dead

Because if it's dead
then so are we.

So the next time
You
You
You

even think or say that our culture
is dead

Remember

We are who and what we remember.

Remember
We come from an over 4,000 year old past
We come from warriors
We come from maga'håga and maga'låhi
We come from a beautiful language
We come from the latte
We come from the roots of trees and the waves of seas
We come from the first people.

So stop saying
our culture
your culture
my culture
is dead.

Because when you say it's dead,
then you're saying that I am dead.

When you say it's dead,
you're saying that I don't exist.

And people,
I'm talking to you
and you
and you

I

exist.

Therefore my culture

Boom boom

Boom boom

Boom boom

IT'S ALIVE!

Nåna

Like the tåsa and haligi of the ancient Chamoru latte stone,
    so, too, does your body   maintain the shape
    of the healthy   Chamoru woman.
    With those   full-figured hips,
    features delivered
through natural birth for generations,
and with those powerful arms,
reaching for the past,   calling on our mañaina,
you have remained strong   throughout the years,
continuously inspire me   to live my culture
allowing me to grow into a young   Chamoru woman myself
Through you,   I have witnessed the persistence
and endurance of my ancestors,   who never failed in constructing a latte.
I gima' taotaomo'na,   the house of the ancient people.
Hågu i acho' latte-ku.   You are my latte stone.

Nu'i Che'lun Palao'an

Like the two lovers,
the sisters tied their hair
and together
they jumped off
Puntan Dos Amantes
into the tåsi,
cleansing themselves
of all
the pain
hurtful words
awkward moments of silence.

In this ocean,
the ocean of their Mother,
they immerse themselves
regaining strength,

Loving each other all over again.

Together
their hair still connected,
they rise quickly through the water
like dolphins
and jump
into the air of their Mother.

Landing back in the ocean,
the sisters
hear:
"It's time to go back.
Nånan Tåno' is calling for you."

Their hair now separated,
the sisters swim back to the land

their Mother.
Laying their bodies to the sand,
they listen to the words of Nånan Tåno':

"Love each other.
Forgive each other.
And always remember
to take care of each other."

Para si Lina'la': Life Lesson #1

Dear Lina'la',
Maila yan ekungok:

Mommy was born a dark-skinned girl
turned darker
whenever I played outside
went to the beach
went to track practice.

And each time I raised my dark brown arm to the
white wall of my bathroom shower
I felt disgusted.

I'd convince myself that dark girls were ugly.

This has got to come off, I'd tell myself as I stood in the shower.

I'd scrub my body so hard,
until my skin turned
not white
but
red.

Mommy just wanted to be light-skinned like
my Korean classmates and my haole classmates
and my fairskinned, beautiful Chamoru classmates
        that all the boys liked.

Often times I found myself being the darkest
of all my classmates.

Even my teachers were white.

Mommy felt left out.

And it didn't help that most people around me would say:
"You're SO dark"
with that tone and look of disgust.

I learned at a young age to hate my chocolate skin
to despise it so much
that after
scrubbing the "dirt" off didn't work,
I would take the advice from my Filipina friends and
buy papaya soap and Nivea lotion from Compadres Mall
to help with the lightening process.

But

nothing

worked.

I was still the dark girl,
the ugly girl.

As I got older
I realized
there was nothing I could do
to be
lighter
whiter.

What annoyed Mommy even more was
whenever people told me to "put on more sunblock"
to "stay out of the sun"
to "just stay inside the house".

Now at 28
I am finally learning to love my chocolate skin.

I am with Daddy, who is also chocolate-skinned.
And he often tells me my chocolate skin is beautiful.

And lately,
people have said that they wish they could have a tan like mine.

But perhaps the biggest compliment of all—
Is that you, Lina'la', are chocolate-skinned

just

like

Mommy.

I want you to grow up loving the color of your skin.

And if ever you come home from school crying because
people teased you about your color

I will hug your brown body tight
And remind you:

That being brown is beautiful.
That brown is the color of the dirt that keeps us grounded in
    our roots.
Brown is the color of our ancestors who worked the land and
    fished at sea.
Brown is the color of the coconut
        an important staple for our people.
Brown is the color of Mommy.

Brown is the color of Daddy.
Brown is the color of your beautiful Pacific Islander body.

Brown is the color of Life.

Don't let anyone convince you
that lighter is
better
more beautiful
that you should play inside
or that you're "too dark".

There is no such thing.

Only the ignorance of those
who don't know
just
how
beautiful
brown
is.

And one more thing, Lina'la':

Don't just be comfortable in your skin.

Be beautiful in it.

Hu guaiya hao.

-si Mommy

Para si Lina'la': Life Lesson #2*

Dear Lina'la':
Maila yan ekungok ta'lo.

When Mommy was growing up,
Nåna and Tåta spoke to me in english.
They rarely spoke to me in Chamoru.

They didn't teach me Chamoru
because they didn't want me
to have an accent
to be inarticulate
to be unsuccessful
or to have trouble in school.

(Little did they know
that by not teaching me Chamoru,
they denied me a big part of who I was.)

Mommy was raised to speak the best english that I could.
I even wrote essays, poems, and stories in english
and often got rewarded
with A's, prizes, and gifts from Nåna and Tåta.

I never questioned how good I
was at speaking and writing in english
or how little Chamoru I knew.

But when Mommy left to Hawai'i for college,
I realized just how important
our language was,
and how if I learned it,

---

* "Para si Lina'la': Life Lesson #1" was published in *Storyboard 15* (2015).

it would be soothing for my soul.*

So I tried to learn as much Chamoru as I could.

But eventually

Life got busy and my effort to become fluent
in Chamoru
became a fleeting one.

Over the years,
Mommy would have these moments
when I would want to be fluent
in Chamoru
and would try to learn it

But each time
those moments would
be overcome by my fear, discomfort, and lack of time.

I had many discussions with people
(like my students)
on the importance of speaking Chamoru
and how it wasn't a dying language.

But while at home, I would ask myself:

*How could I expect the language
not to die with them
when it was already dying with me?*

---

* Reference to Dr. Sharleen Santos-Bamba's interview in the documentary
"Mothering Guahan", where she said, "English is how we get through life; it is
not what soothes the soul." (Therefore, one could imply that for Chamorus, it is
our Chamoru language that soothes our souls.)

As time went on,
my desire to be fluent in Chamoru
remained

but I just found it easier,
more convenient,

to use english.

But I wouldn't tell anyone.

Because whenever I talked to my students
and sent emails to people,
I would greet them with a "Håfa Adai"
and use as much broken Chamoru as I could

So people could believe that I was actually making an effort.

And then Lina'la',
Neni-hu,
you came along.

And there was this immense urgency for fluency
in Chamoru

Because you are Chamoru.
Mommy and Daddy are Chamoru.
Our Ancestors are Chamoru.

You have to learn the language of our ancestors,
the words that connect us to our past
the language that you will share

with your children
so that they can be connected to our past.

It has been said that the Chamoru language
will be gone from this Earth
in 20 years.

So neni-hu:
You will learn Chamoru,
because it is your responsibility
your cultural obligation
to keep giving it life
to speak it and write it
every day
so that it will continue to thrive
so that our ancestors will be kept alive
so that our culture will continue to be a gift to this world.*

So that one day:
We won't have to hear people say that our language is dying
That our culture is dying.

So that one day,
You will be able to tell stories
write poetry
and leave life lessons for your children

Without hesitation
without fear
without discomfort:

---

* In a lecture I attended by Dr. Unaisi Nabobo-Baba, she mentioned that our indigenous cultures and languages are our gifts to the world and that if we had no culture or language to share, then "what gift would we have to share with the world"?

gi Fino' Chamoru.

Hu guaiya hao.

-si Mommy

Re-Gaining Senses (Honiara, Guadalcanal: July 10, 2012)

As I sit under a thatched-roof hut,
listening to the birds chirping
taking in the smells of
burning sage
mosquito coils
the distant ocean
the lunch from the dining hall
the aftermath of the pouring rain

I think of my home

and how the only birds I can hear
are the ones that don't fly
the ones that wake me up every morning
with their crows and their flapping wings.

When did the birds lose their chirp?

Was it when the Spanish anchored their ships on our shores?
Was it when the U.S. navy raised its country's flag?
Was it when the Japanese beheaded our people?

When did the smell of the ocean
become unfamiliar
distant
foreign?

Was it when Santa Marian Kamalen trekked to Malesso' on the backs
    of crabs?
Was it when the latte were bulldozed and replaced by 15-story, 2-star
    hotels?
Was it when our pastimes became times of our past
        no longer living in the present?

As I sit under this thatched-roof hut
watching the locals start their 30-minute walk for the day
listening to the drum beats from Tahiti
and the laughs of my people in the dorms
feeling the raindrops on my skin

I think of my home

and how so much needs to change.

So that we can:

Hear our paluma chirping
Recognize our tåsi waving
See our niyok flowing

And feel our home

Enveloping us
in her love.

Re-Occupation Day a.k.a. "Liberation Day"

Every 21st of July,
      the people of Guåhan march in their red, white, and blue,
      thanking Uncle Sam and his men in uniform.

The Chamoru people lived through
      over 300 years of forced Catholicism
         and forced last names,
      bowing to Yokois
         and forced death marches,
   and they continue to be enslaved
      by the SPAM-crazed golden arches,
      by drafts and recruitments,
      by "the land of the free."

I tano' i taotao-hu på'go iyo-ñiha—

They took Sumay
      and used it for their military.
They made us citizens
      but denied us the vote.
They stole our language
      and made us speak English.

Our leaders say that we're free,
that we're making good money from the military
and tourism.

As I drive through Tomhom,
my view of the ocean obstructed
      by the Outrigger and the Hyatt,
I think of the stories Tåta used to tell me
about the latte stone huts that once lined the ocean
and how they were bulldozed
to keep up with the times.

"No Trespassing" signs now line much of our lands and ocean.

I taotao-hu trabiha ti manlibre:

My people are not free.

Sandals

In 1976, Auntie Maria and Uncle Juan
    danced the cha cha for the first time.
She was in her red shoes;
    he was in his yori.

Every Friday,
even after their shoes wore out,
Auntie Maria and Uncle Juan still danced.

Red shoes are dancing shoes.

But Uncle Juan died last week.

People at the funeral,
in their black clothes and their black shoes,
couldn't stop crying over the man—
    who made them kadun mannok,
    taught them how to use a kamyu,
    and told them stories:
        how the two lovers jumped off the cliff,
        how Sirena turned into a mermaid,
        how the flame tree got its flames.

Red shoes are dancing shoes, not funeral shoes.

At the burial,
Auntie Maria danced her way up
to the casket
in her red heels.

They watched her
    take off her red heels
    and place them
        on top of the red roses

that covered Uncle Juan's casket—

"Until we dance again," she said,

"Hu guaiya hao."

Sitting in History

Do you know what it's like to sit in a history class
    listening to your professor talk about his history
my history
your history
our history?

Do you know what it's like to sit in a history class
    listening to your professor talk about what life was like
For your ancestors
    before the Spanish came
        Chanting, Fishing
        Latte, Lusong
        Amot
    when the Spanish came
        cross, bible
        clothes, church
        baptism
    after the Spanish . . . left (but never really did)

Do you know what it's like to sit in a history class
    listening to your professor talk about one colonizer
        after the other
    Countries that hung their flags
        and told our people that we were under their control
        Us not knowing that we would lose control of
everything we knew
    Our people's ways of living were forever altered
        tainted by the colonizers' (plural)
bibles, crosses, churches, SPAM, chocolate, McDonald's, militarism

Do you know what it's like to sit in a history class
    Not wanting to listen to your professor talk about
    the tragedies of your people
        how the Spanish came

and killed THEM
how the Japanese came
and killed THEM
how the Americans came
and killed US

I know what it's like to sit in my history class
    listening to my professor talk about
    our people
    our past

I know what it's like to sit in my history class
and feeling
on some days,
like I don't want to be here

Listening

But on most days,
feeling
like
I am being reconnected
    to my ancestors
    to my past

I know what it's like to sit in my history.

I'm sitting in it right now.

To the Peoples of Nations under U.S. Occupation:

I come from a land,
a small island,
lined with fences
where my people
are used to looking
at the lands of our ancestors
through

holes.

I come from a people,
a colonized people,
lined with wrinkles,
deeply entrenched canyons
displayed on their faces,
each red vein in their bloodshot eyes
leading to a time of
death
struggle
War.

One day, we will all be free.
Our nations will no longer be confined
by guns,
fences,
and national security.

But until then,
if ever we forget why we're in our struggles,
there will be

"No Trespassing" signs to remind us.

Walking through Tomhom

I had a dream last night.
I was walking through the jungle,
and as I passed each tree,
it collapsed right beside me.
The ground was dug up,
the naked raw earth exposed.

How could this happen—
to our tåno'
to our mañaina
to our manggåfa
to us?

The big strong tronkon nunu
the taotaomo'na hid in
were no more.

I screamed,
tears numbing my
blood red face.

As I walked
through the naked earth,
my body weakened.

I fell to the ground,
my palms touching
        the unfamiliar earth,
my eyes searching
        for the old tronkon nunu,
my ears open
        to the calling of our mañaina.

I didn't know this earth.

I couldn't see the trees.
But
in the distance,
I could hear:

"Munga ma'åñao, hagå-hu.
Munga ma'åñao.
Ti bai in dingu hao."

"It's okay, our daughter.
It's okay.
We will never leave you."

MAI KA PŌ MAI KA ʻOIAʻIʻO

Jamaica Heolimeleikalani Osorio

HĀNAU

Hānau Hawaiʻi he Moku

When i awake
i am cold at the center
Some of my edges cool from the chill of the pacific
i feel a stillness settling in the water
i wonder how long i might be alone
Until i feel a quake
Something has changed
i am no longer the only infant to this ocean
ʻAʻole

There is a sister
Her head turned away
i see only the bridge of her back
i cry out to her
Hoping to carry her name on my lips
Hoping to bridge this blue between us
She does not stir

All at once i remember the calm
silence before her
how this quiet is not the same
seeing her makes it lonelier

another shake cracks at the base of my chest
he is long
red edges bleeding into the sea
I worry for the dark ring around him

1, 2, 3, and then more are born
they all remain
silent
the ocean calms
and i am alone
learning the depth of pō

Kumulipo

What happens to the ones forgotten
the ones who shaped my heart from their rib cages?
i want to taste the tears in their names
trace their souls into my vocal chords so that i can feel related again
because i have forgotten my own grandparents middle names
Forgotten what color thread god used to sew me together with

There is a culture
Somewhere beneath my skin that i've been searching for since i
    landed here
But it's hard to feel sometimes
Because at Stanford we are innovative
the city of Macintosh breeds thinkers of tomorrow
and i have forgotten how to remember

But our roots cannot remember themselves
Cannot remember how to dance if we don't chant for them
And will not sing unless we are listening
but our tongues feel too foreign in our own mouths
we don't dare speak out loud
and we, cant even remember our own parents names
so who will care to remember mine if i don't teach them

i want to teach my future children
how to spell family with my middle name—Heolimeleikalani
how to hold love with Kamakawiwoʻole
how to taste culture in the Kumulipo
please
do not forget me
my father
Kamakawiwoʻole
who could not forget his own
Leialoha
do not forget what's left

cuz this is all we have
and you wont find our roots online

We have no dances or chants if we have no history
just rants
no roots
just tears
this is all i have of our family history
and now its yours
'O Ma'alolaninui ke kāne 'o Lonokaumakahiki ka wahine, noho pū lāua
a hānau 'ia 'o Imaikalani he kāne. 'O Imaikalani ke kāne 'o Keko'okalani
ka wahine, noho pū lāua a hānau 'ia 'o Pa'auluhi Kahinuonālani he
kāne. 'O Pa'aluhi Kahinuonālani ke kāne 'o Pi'ipi'i Keali'iwaiwai'ole ka
wahine, noho pū lāua ma Hāwī Kohala a hānau 'ia 'o Charles Moses
Kamakawiwo'oleokamehameha he kāne.

'O Hainaloa ke kāne 'o Niau ka wahine, noho pū lāua a hānau 'ia 'o
Kaluaihonolulu he wahine. 'O Kaluaihonolulu ka wahine 'o Nako'oka
ke kāne, noho pū lāua a hānau 'ia 'o Kapahu he wahine. 'O Kapahu
ka wahine 'o Kua ke kāne, noho pū lāua ma Koholālele a hānau 'ia 'o
Daisy Keali'i'ai'awa'awa he wahine.

'O Charles Moses Kamakawiwo'oleokamehameha ke kāne 'o Daisy
Keali'iai'awa'awa ka wahine, noho pū lāua ma Hāmākua a hānau 'ia
'o Eliza Leialoha Kamakawiwo'ole he wahine. 'O Eliza Leialoha Ka-
makawiwo'ole ka wahine 'o Emil Montero Osorio ke kāne, noho pū lāua
ma Hilo a hānau 'ia 'o Elroy Thomas Leialoha Osorio he kāne.

'O Manūawai ke kāne 'o Keao ka wahine, noho pū lāua ma Kohala a
hānau 'ia 'o Sarah Pi'ikea Papanui he wahine. 'O Sarah Pi'ikea Papanui
ka wahine 'o Kam Sheong Akiona ke kāne, noho pū lāua a ma Kona
Hema a hānau 'ia 'o Nani Kaluahine Kimoe Akiona he wahine. 'O
Nani Kaluahine Kimoe Akiona ka wahine 'o LeRoy Adam Anthony
Kay ke kāne, noho pū lāua ma Kaimukī a hānau 'ia 'o Clara Ku'ulei

Kay he wahine.

'O Elroy Thomas Leialoha Osorio ke kāne 'o Clara Ku'ulei Kay ka
wahine, noho pū lāua ma Hilo a hānau 'ia 'o Jonathan Kay Kamakaw-
iwo'ole Osorio he kāne

'O William Dunne ke kāne 'o Margaret Davis ka wahine, noho pū
lāua ma Queens Ireland a hānau 'ia 'o James Dunne he kāne. 'O James
Dunne ke kāne 'o Mary Farrell ka wahine, noho pū lāua a hānau 'ia
'o John Christopher Dunne he Kāne. 'O John Christopher Dunne
ke kāne 'o Sarah Evelyn Vogt ka wahine, noho pū lāua a hānau 'ia 'o
Edward Lawrence Dunn he kāne. 'O Edward Lawrence Dunn ke kāne
'o Genevieve Catherine Offer ka wahine, noho pū lāua ma Royal Oak
Michigan a hānau 'ia 'o Mary Carol Dunn he wahine

'O Jonathan Kay Kamakawiwo'ole Osorio ke kāne 'o Mary Carol
Dunn ka wahine. Noho pū lāua ma Pālolo a hānai 'ia o Kāneali'i
Kamakawiwo'oleokamehameha he kāne, hānau ia 'o Duncan Andrew
Kamakanaonākuahiwi Osorio he kāne, hānau 'ia 'o Jamaica Heolime-
leikalani Osorio he wahine, hānau ia 'o Hali'aku'uleialohaonālani Kīka-
haikalāhikilehuau'i Osorio he wahine, hānai 'ia 'o Lehuanani Alana
Pilipa'a Osorio he wahine, hānai ia 'o Kalehua Kalili Osorio he wahine.

do not forget us
mai poina

'Āpuakenui: Kailua's Finest

'Āpuakenui is licking her lips across Koʻolau's spine
And i watch as their Uhi falls down her curves and floods the
   muliwai

'Āpuakenui is tracing her fingers across the open shell of a crowning
   tsunami
And i am a recollection dissolving
Trying to (re)member the way you and i once shaped moana

'Āpuakenui is flooding light into the breeching bay of Heʻeia
Catching ʻOama between the webs of her toes
And i am holding my ea at the base of this Manawa
Waiting for your ʻOpihi lips to bring me home

'Āpuakenui is shaking the ʻōpua free from her seaweed hair
Shaping sky for her promiscuous arc
And i am two palms opened to akua
Trying to catch the iʻa that fall from her scalp

'Āpuakenui is crying
Wailing for a lover who won't return
And i am drenched with longing for you

E kuʻu hoa ʻōpua o Hōpoe,

Not even all this beauty
Shedding itself around me
misting this palapalai
Can distract from my longing for your lips
Sweet like the iwi of ʻopihi
After the tongue's first taste

KINO PĀPĀLUA

Kaona

Co-Authored by Ittai Wong

Ua ola ka ʻōlelo i ka hoʻoili ʻana o nā pua
Our language survived through the passing of flowers
In 1896
The last reigning monarch of Hawaiʻi,
Queen Liliʻuokalani was
Held prisoner in her own palace
Communication with the outside world was prohibited
Thus newspapers were snuck into her room wrapped around flowers
For months our Queen and her people wrote songs and stories
Hidden in Hawaiian,
So as to converse without the Overthrowing Provisional government
   knowing

It is because of this we know our history
The language of hidden meanings
Kaona,
The first written Hawaiian poetry
Songs and dance were the medium in which we decoded their
Denotation
Connecting connotation through
Kaona
Speaking of flowers but meaning children
Ua maikaʻi ke kalo i ka ʻohā
The branch is a reflection of the taro root
We are a reflection of our genesis
The most intricate euphemisms that ever existed

And you had to understand the history and culture
To decrypt this language
Had to dig deeper than dictionaries
Beneath esophagus
And vocal cords
To grasp the root of the words our people would chant

Just to understand their messages

This is kaona,
In a time when our freedom of speech was denied
And words needed to be hidden in order to be heard
The language of commonality was no longer an option
So our oral traditions evolved or else words would die

Our language survived through the passing of flowers	Ua ola ka ʻōlelo i ka hoʻoili ʻana o nā pua
Our ancestors survived through the passing of tongues	Ua ola nā iwi i ka hoʻoili ʻana o ka ʻōlelo
A dying language wrapped a dying culture	Ua ʻōwili ʻia ka mākou keiki me ka ʻōlelo
Our flowers	Nā Pua
Our Children	Nā Pua
The ones we promised to die for weren't surviving	Ke moe i ka make nei ka mākou mau keiki
So we sent our stories	No laila ua hoʻoili mākou nā moʻolelo
Wrapped our children in blankets of words	Wahī nā keiki me nā kapa o nā ʻōlelo
Hoping they hold on to their meanings	Manaʻolana mākou e paʻa ʻana lākou i nā manaʻo

E hō mai ka ʻike mai luna mai ē
ʻO nā mea hūnā noʻeau
ʻO nā mele
E hō mai
E hō mai
E hō mai ē

So today i pray
For the winds to blow understanding to her people upon the backs of
  change
i pray
That forgotten stories everywhere flood through
Like the white washed ships
Which stripped our language away.
i pray.
For every foreign tongue
Re-learn its native kiss in language
Formed as flowers,
Spread across the lands we know as our own
Hold the salvation of our souls
Through the wishes begot long ago
Because some meanings should never be hidden
And with every word lost,
We lose a piece of ourselves
With every story forgot,
We lose a piece of our history

It's time to uncover the past that we may understand our future
Interpret our stories that we may better know ourselves
So listen to me

Existence persists as long as we have language
If we cannot communicate with each other, we cannot survive
He mana kō ka leo, a inā 'a'ohe leo, 'a'ohe ola
Without language,
We have nothing

We must see to it that our language survives like the past, through
  flowers
Ua ola ka 'ōlelo i ka ho'oili 'ana o nā pua

E hiki nā pua e ola i ka hoʻoili ʻana o ka ʻōlelo
So our children can survive,
Through the passing of language

ʻŌlelo Hawaiʻi

their eyes widen when the water falls out
ocean spilling vowels through me
kaona spurting from the salt
classmates stutter in silence
trying to repeat
sound locked in their shackle shaped lips

they do not know
the way their english barely breaches the surface
and i find it ironic
that i have been chosen
an artist in a mode
dictated by the superficiality of colonial tongues

for the first time in over four years
i find myself isolated by translation
remembering how comfortable i am in this crater
laying my body in the curve of Haumea's tongue
and yet, in contrast
how self conscious i have become of my presentation
and the way the others gaze
scopophilia spilling from the iridescence of their irises
making me sculpture like
walls building around me, a museum

until i am still again
silent
letting only the english
breach the crest

Moving Target

My body, on the day I learned to remember, became a labyrinth of secrets.
—Chinaka Hodge

1.

the day my mother promised me the gravity
of the moon was the day i found my body
was meant to be an ocean
but was only a hollow shark skin drum
only pillars of stories that never stuck
a belly that would never swell, tides
that never pulled, mountains
I couldn't conjure, scars
where hips should have been, beauty
was the lie our mothers told to us in tradition
and truth was a story that left
a bitter taste
like sour poi on our tongue

2.

Everything was brown when i was born
Family was a gradient ocean that was too wide to understand
but by age 6
my eyes learned to polarize and measure
I learned the difference between mother and father
was a continent
and 15 points on a chromatic scale
I knew then
I would spend the rest of my life
Trying to fit into the craters crumbling between them

our skin tone kept us
quiet
from questioning these bodies
wondering which parts were broken
we learned to be
complacent in our difference
while we soaked in the silence
let the salt seep into our skeleton
leave its mark
make us feel like we belonged to the ocean

ŌLAʻI

Green Washing and White Dollar Policy

In Hawai'i
our catastrophes
flood in on warnings
geographically isolated and not partial to shifting plates
we are accustomed to the disasters
that come in the wake of another's tragedy

1960
Chile shakes herself awake
and Hawai'i finds herself
Crumbling under the whitewash spit
South America's broken
Brown bodies come
crashing into our sand skin
we put salt in the wound
kick her while she is down

2010
Chile crumbles again
buildings shift like rubble
tumble down the streets of scarcity
Her scars keep a quiet secret
Middle class America watches the death toll increase
we blame poor infrastructure and tectonic plate anger
Forget the greed that leaves brown children
Swept under a growing pillar called poverty
Prefer not to think of the burden that strained shoulders are expected
    to carry
When the policy of white money
Increases "high efficiency" and "hybrid" tax write offs
Greed and profit maximization is not mentioned
as the world forgets
hunger

is a dark body
crying

So we find Chile's regret
cracked and caved into a corner
while Hawai'i curls into her sirens
waits for the tide to recede and heads for the mountains
we find ourselves praying for the disaster to strike no further
thanking our gods for
protocol
and the time to be warned

2012 is no different
the world economies fall like the lip of a tsunami
Japan curls back like silly putty
and Hawai'i wakes to the morning tide rising

And today in 2014
A small community town on the island of Hawai'i
whose name lacks the shimmer and economic opportunity of Waikīkī
coils herself awake past the breech of a hurricane
Puna shakes herself in disbelief
While on Mauna Kea,
Poli'ahu softens under the abominations a Fake State has erected in
    the name of "science"
Chasing the luster of stars at any cost
looking for answers to the world's heaviest questions
Forgetting our oldest promise lies beneath our feet
So Pele
Our eldest sister of fire assures her kānaka a homecoming worth
    remembering
First she sends the tremors
Then Hi'iaka's green hips retract under the tracks of her mo'opuna's
    sins

Our emerald turns an island a shade of darkened repurposed sheet
    metal,
The ʻāina beneath us melting

All the while
the government cries about the increase of natural disasters and their
    effect on an insecure visitor economy
the suits worry for the lost dollars but
No one speaks for the families
Rooted 2000 generations deep
in my islands
Instead, we attempt to soften these cavernous bodies into utility
allow our ʻāina to be fracked by GMO farming
and Geothermal drilling
how many gods will we defile before we are abandoned
how many times will we proclaim that we are here to protect the
    earth and yet forget her name?

I've seen far too much environmentalism take place
from the safety of our titanium cocoons
Insisting we can handle this heat of consequence
Penning policy and finding comfort in our distance
Forgetting the brown bodies forged into the spine of this story
We write off our environmental impact in dollars
While Chile's children are fossilized for a new generation of green
    washing
Japan's future forgotten under tsunami curl and a nuclear reactor's
    venomous spit

And then there are the lesser known of Oceania
Our sea of islands
Children born in the Marshalls
Unable to swim faster than a rising sea
I wonder,

Have you heard their stories?
How young families
With old histories stand on the shore of their fear
Measuring their future as the ocean sprouts wings
How they can actually see the sea growing
And my brothers and sisters in Fiji
Fighting for the right to not have every bit of their precious minerals
    mined from the depths of their bellies

And who of us has not diverted our eyes from any portion of these
    disasters
Too many of us are silent when environmental issues devastate brown
    spaces
This privileged arrogance is deafening
While there are genealogies fighting for a chance to speak
Our first world dollar offers the white noise of blockbusters to co-opt
    indigenous tragedy

And yet the crying voices continue
Vocal chorded sirens insisting that in Oceania
the land and ocean are intrinsically linked to our bodies
we watch as all three have been written over and retold
a silencing practice called erasure
a exercise in history, the victorious call forgetting
what a privilege this selective memory
parading the freedom of ignorance like a present

So I'm writing my portion of this story
Of the displaced, evicted and forgotten
Hoping to (re)member the small shards left that i've been able to
    carry
Making a statement about the intersection of it all
Trying to trace this piko towards a solution

An Umbilical chord binding us not only to the world's natural
   resources but to each other
And making each of us implicit in this social justice disaster
From the stripped rain forest just beyond the shores of Australia in
   PNG
To the deep sea mining off the coast of Fiji
to Puna's scorched spine
and Chile's cracked lips
Hawai'i's biocultural prostitution
And Guahan's military base hips

It is time we stop congratulating our collective silence and see
How we've wounded our already weak
by ignoring that every bit of this trauma is connected
This is not a matter of provocative speech and liberal action
This is a world drowning in its own backwash and arrogance
The mostly white and wealthy brace behind the brown sandbags of
   the world's broken
Evaluate the damage of another thousand dead and displaced brown
   bodies
The suited statistician takes down the toll with biodegradable
   materials
Insisting he is a part of the solution
Clinging shamelessly to the backs of the planet's darkest poor
Praying to his recyclable god
to be spared

Kāne Kōlea

He comes to take
His feathers growing
dark silk wraps his marbling sides
leaving
without a thought
to the poʻowai
now dry
the craters carved under his claws
the god choking concrete he leaves behind

He does not cut the mouth
while sucking the last bit of sap from his spurs
i watch; wishing him that scarring lesson

while he departs
whole,
my ʻāina cavernous
summits stolen
rivers dry
and renamed
He leaves, full
having emptied this ʻāina
mauka a makai
we are left with a foreign landscape
unfamiliar to our akua
and
I curse the patience of karma

Warm Welcoming Fire

I cannot write
another name / the once living body, sunken
I cannot stand
the weight, another brown son is
hanging / i cannot breathe
this generation's inheritance
the choking stench of violence persists
this accumulated death of the innocent

so instead i watch as we take
up
the pens and signs
throw our hands
up
the voices
and prayer
up
we open
our palms crying
please

don't shoot

//

count the syllables and cities who home the buried
who mourn the dead and dying
whose breath is held
still waiting
for Justice

count the times
we have witnessed the master's call for massacre
held our young and black closer
shielding our children from this wildfire

of cold slaughter turned acquittal

    remember the young men / vanishing
    remember America's promise
    kept secret from their opened / disappearing hands

    Today we light this foundation
    that allows for the protection of the killing
    and the dishonor of the dying
    we burn with the skin and bones of our children
    black
    dead
    but not forgotten
    begging

    //

    what will change this country
    if not a young man
    shot porous
    his open palms'
    broken promise
    his burial's
    warm welcoming fire

HULIHIA

Hōpoe i ka Poli o Hiʻiaka

Many men have told my story
have uttered your name into speech
some have carved it into pōhaku and pepa
a part of
you and i live forever in the margins between sound and solid
but no man
no woman
or soul
no body has written or known the words we shared

those parts of us were only held in kino
in leo
now
stay carved in the creases of my poho
so that every part of this earth i hold has a moment to know your
    touch
reminding me that
ʻae,
maybe our words are best kept for two
but the manner in which you glided over and danced with papa
    deserves to be shouted from my hallowed hands

I will resist
the letting go of the ocean that tries to fall through
even when i am tempted to destroy this temple
allow feelings to rise like tides
swell the fractures at the base of my ʻōpū
hollow a crater once full of fire
transform kīlauea's heat into a forgotten story
instead i choose to
hold so tight these hua
our only pua
that they may lay in the center of my poli
a place once reserved for aliʻi

but ahi and ʻā have left me an open cavity for your memory
I promise
that those parts of you we shared in quiet
they will not spill open

It is right that only this earth knows of the words we planted
that they lay rooted in the kumu of our moʻo
only my gift of lehua can ever claim our love
it is right
even if they too are gone now

Not an Apology

i watched as you witnessed the burning
rage swelling in your piko
You feel yourself   astray
When rage makes us the same

My love for you has always resulted in fire
we came here   i made a path for you
prepared this land for your lehua
for your 'ami with that girl

How has your memory failed you
to expect any response other than this burning
that you could leave   and that i might allow this 'āina to
refuse my reflection

You were gone.   What else am i to do but birth mountains?

You want to blame this flame
to curse this kumu 'ahi
but it is born of your skin
I burn only for you

but you refuse my offering of tinder
want to bury me in ocean
kino nalo i ka nalu
crack the papa of this lua

You are of me
this poli   all heat
 no part of
you can reject me

[77]

I am your body
my anger is yours and
for you,　　　　　always.
do not dig here for a mihi

you have earned no apologies
sister.　　　　　it was your mistake
to expect different　　　this is the way
I have always loved you

Hawaiʻi Ponoʻī

It's 1872
David Kalākaua—not yet crowned
not yet anointed or kinged
Pens a song at the request of Kamehameha V, Lota Kapuāiwa
Hawaiʻi Ponoʻī
A new national anthem
A new symbol of strength
A new promise for Hawaiians of Kalākaua's generation,
that like those before
they would stand and fight for their right to noho Aupuni
Today we call this resistance
Then,
they called it pono

Hawaiʻi ponoʻī
Nānā i kou mōʻī
Ka lani aliʻi,
Ke aliʻi

So as Kalākaua writes
we sing of generations of makaʻāinana & mōʻī
who offered their fierce bodies
for this legacy
we sing
And remember we are the sons and daughters of pō
The deepest and darkest most creative force of this world
We sing
And remember Umialiloa, Kihapiilani, Manono and Kekuaokalani
Kānaka Maoli who practiced
strength, resiliency and resistance,
knowing NO human power was so supreme that it could not or
    should not be overturned when unjust

Kalākaua writes

And remembers an older Kamehameha
Kauikeaouli thundering, Ua mau ke ea o ka ʻāina i ka pono
Kalākaua holds this in his iwi,
holds its promise in his melodies
as we've been taught to hold it in our bloodline,
cradle it on our tongues,
keep it sacred and safe from the poisoned fingertips of this fake state

It's 1893
An overthrown kingdom
a lāhui in distress:
Ellen Kehoʻohiwaokalani Wright Prendergast feeds
her generations with rocks of resistance
gives us a melodic reminder
of our genealogy of protest
& Kaluaikoʻolau and his family
run through brush at Kalalau on Kauaʻi.
Their steps are heavy, but precise,
Because they know the weight of generations of oppression shrouding
    their shoulders
they realize the power from which they resist

They refuse to be wrongfully imprisoned for his sickness,
And there is no regret for resistance.
When Piʻilani buries him,
her tears return his body and rifle to dust.
His generation's ihe,
an answer strapped across his bare chest,
pointing back to Kalākaua's call to protect THIS legacy

> *Makua lani ē,*
> *Kamehameha ē,*
> *Na kaua e pale,*
> *Me ka ihe*

It's January 7, 1895
Over three hundred men,
led by Robert Wilcox,
take cover in pōhaku above Leʻahi
with rifles armed with gunpowder and aloha ʻāina
Untrained soldiers give their lives for Hawaiʻi.
These are not the koa of the kīpuʻupuʻu rain of Waimea.
They are only the last physical defense of people,
who know in their naʻau that laying down
to the opposition is not an option.
Though they are not ihe
—not malo—not maʻa,
they are the kaua who answer Kalākaua's call.

It's 1897
When America's physical power is a muscle that cannot be matched
Kānaka Maoli of the patriotic league take to the greatest weapon of
    this new time:
Paper & pen
Our kūpuna's names scratched
into a new kind of pōhaku
painting a picture of a strong, unified people
—A nation
whose love for ʻāina
& lāhui could not be rivaled
erased
or buried.
Under joint resolution

Hawaiʻi ponoʻī
Nānā i nā aliʻi
Nā pua muli kou
Nā pākiʻi

It's January 3, 1976
After almost six decades of mourning
nine young Kānaka Maoli
galvanized by the resistance to Kalama Valley evictions
land on Kahoʻolawe
Kohe Mālamalama o Kanaloa.
They come to heal the scars
of an island torn by the bombs
of someone else's war
for someone else's security.
On that day, the PKO reignited
a practice of aloha ʻāina so powerful
it defeated the largest Navy in the world.

Between March 6th and 7th 1977
George Helm and Kimo Mitchell,
two members of the PKO, were taken
Their sacrifice reminds us what
we must be willing to offer back to our lāhui.
Sometimes
we do not return on our own two feet.
Sometimes
we are only
the song
the promise
the faint memory of a sweet melody
the moʻolelo for the next generation to carry.

And carry we have
On January 17, 1993
We gathered at the palace to hear a brilliant Kanaka Maoli mana
    wahine, Haunani-Kay Trask proclaim,
"We are not american, we are not american, we are not american, We
    will die as Hawaiians, we will never be americans"

Now it's 2015
those of us who remain
have the kuleana their lessons laced
into the backbone of our practice.
So they shall never be forgotten.

> *Hawai'i pono'ī*
> *E ka lāhui ē*
> *'O kāu hana nui*
> *E ui ē*

This is our anthem of resistance
written from the inspiration of past promises.

On March 29, 2015
Aloha 'Āina of this generation
ascend our sacred Mauna a Wākea
they stay through the night
defending our sacred piko on the front lines and the courtrooms ever
    since

Their sacrifice confirms resistance as a Hawaiian tradition.
'Ai pōhaku:
as fundamental to our story
as hula and oli.
This is the mo'olelo of Hawai'i
of new roots sprouting from old seeds,

e nā po'e o Hawai'i
'ōnipa'a in this resistance knowing our kūpuna:

[83]

Robert Wilcox, George Helm, Kaluaikoʻolau, Manono, Haunani-Kay
    Trask
and the hundreds of thousands
who joined in their sacrifice
would stand with our brothers and sisters
between our sacred mauna and this desecration
until the very last Aloha ʻĀina . . .
We stand on their shoulders today
when we insist on a better future
we honor their names.

So come
sing with us
know you are joined
by the generations
who sang these stories before you.
Know in your naʻau
that this is the way we rise.

> *Makua lani ē,*
> *Kamehameha ē,*
> *Na kaua e pale,*
> *Me ka ihe*

SERETAGI

Tagi Qolouvaki

Tell Me a Story
(for uncle Talanoa)

He vows I am planted beneath the Frangipani
Promises I am seeded beneath the Bua.

He has his father's tongue,
Owns his mother's languages.
They sing honeyed songs together.
He has even tamed the palagi one—
It rides his tongue
And he is fertile with story.

Deftly, he weaves tales
Like the finest mats
Constructs memories
Tapa-tapestries
Stained in soil and
Colored with song.

We store them,
Cultural currency for the next birth
Death and wedding.
We carry them
To make us
Real.

He is a teller of tall tales, Talanoa

But what are stories if not lies
Though sweet as vakalolo
Cleaved to our fingers
Floating our souls
In the fat of coconut?

What are memories if not construction:
       The storyteller as tattooist
       Marking,
       And not marking,
       Brown skin.

       And They say
       If your pito-pito is unplanted
           You will wander
       They say
       If it is unplanted
           Home will elude you

       Well mine is buried in story
       Planted in a tall tale
       And I wander
       Yes,
       And home is a story
       Home is a story where the Frangipani flowers.

For Nico

how do i describe
how my body wakes, moves
to the heat of your words . . .
like pele's footprints waken kīlauea.
your words so hot they're molten
syllables slip and slide, thickly,
stir my depths
shift plates between our nations
send your seas against my shores.
your tongue, your vowels,
so deep i ride waves against and through them
my skin becomes your ocean
your blood my tide . . .

i tattoo you with teeth and nails
dreams and tongue;
tattoo you deeply
stories old and new
into the skin of my heart
in indigo, in ink,
with shell lip and coral dust
memory and desire . . .
i will trace lines
undulating
spiraling
reaching
like our bodies for each other . . .
yes, deeply
into skin
lips, tongue and breath, till
my scent becomes yours
your texture mine

your words

quicken
> my blood-tissue-cells

> like pele
> i am ready
> to birth new islands
> darken fresh soil
> with this love . . .

> we will grow frangipani
> with creamy yellow centers
> papaya and blue taro
> sugarcane and mangoes
> . . . with this love

Masu

"'Tiko can't be developed,' Manu declared, 'unless the ancient gods are killed.'"
—Epeli Hau'ofa, *Tales of the Tikongs*

Dua

Where do the gods we've forgotten go?
To Burotu?
Did they slip into the skin of the new god?
Do they sleep
in the qele ni vanua
Awaiting our remembering
we, na lewe ni vanua
the flesh of the earth
their descendants?

Where are all our bete, na dautadra
our priests and priestesses?
Do they slumber in the archives
records of ritual
and ethnographic portraiture?
Do they live in the vuniwai
prescribing roots and medicinal herbs
to remove sorcery, heal hearts and other wounds?
How do we supplicate the gods without
their bodies, mouths, ears as mediums
na wa vicovico between us?

Rua

Karlo once said, "the gods are in your marrow"
and the words have settled deep
like kava sediment
na yalo ni vanua   the earth's soul
in the base of the tanoa.

Kalou gata, Kalou vu
     Degei, Dakuwaqa, Daucina,
     is that you, coiled in the heart of my bones?
     Your breath what moves my blood?

     If our dead are woven into our flesh
     like the music of bone flutes
     perhaps it is we who lie dormant;
     flesh of the vanua
     asleep to the divine
     Rocked to unconsciousness
     by the seductions and threats of new gods

     Tolu

     Capell's *New Fijian dictionary*
     defines Kalou gata
     as "blessed, happy; happiness
     and *formerly* a mode of worship rendered to Degei."
     Kalou gata literally translates to
     snake god.
     "Kalou," the new god inhabits you now
     but Degei is as old as the land
     the root of his body is vatu
     stone

     Va

     Degei
     you who live in the sweet juice of our bones,
     you who birthed our people
     from Turukawa's eggs
     kept warm under your watch,
     you who made a home for the first people

in the arms of the Vesi tree,
you who taught us how to grow and cook
the kakana dina
the true food of the land

Kalou gata, Kalou vu
we your children
face futures without fish
and shores that creep steadily inland.
You, god of the mountains
cave-dweller,
we open our eyes
we bring dalo, ika, puaka, vonu
and yaqona
remember us

Suka

"More than 26,000 fish and other marine species in Honolulu Harbor suffocated and died as the molasses spread and sank to the ocean floor about 5 miles west of Waikiki's hotels and beaches. The spill happened in an industrial area of Honolulu Harbor west of downtown, where Matson loads molasses and other goods for shipping." —AP

Dua

May your fossil fuel blood-
lines shrivel in
the heat of Maui's
noonday sun.

May the he'e that is your war-
machine be lured by
the cowrie bait
of Oceania's fishermen
and women
for meat
on our children's tables.

May your dollar-
bill idols leap with
you to Burotu.

May you choke
on your high-fructose
corn syrup
molasses
and GMOs
over breakfast
lunch
and afternoon teas
till you know
the pain of Papa.

May Tangaloa
dream you
a million deaths

and Hinenuitepō
refuse you
the dark and cool embrace
of earth's
children.

Rua

How do we
survive stolen

    children?

gunned down
indigenous men?

molasses
spills that drown

    our fish?

How do we
love sugar

as it strangles
the breath of

    Moana Nui?

Tolu

My bubu lived for sugar;
every day she ladled
four tablespoons
into her ceylon tea
over her quaker oats
and coconut rice.

Sugar made her smile
wide and toothless
for tea and porridge
may be eaten
without dentures.

Sugar brought war
between the matriarchs
of my family;
my bubu and my mother
raging at each other
over the dining table
as we cut
her sugar intake in half
then whole
in concern
for her failing health.

Sugar made her scheme
borrow small containers
of crude brown
from the neighbors
much poorer
than we.

Sugar makes my mother and I
weep
as we continue to
miss her
and remember how we denied
her pleasures

but my bubu also loved fish
cawaki, nama, yaga . . .

I imagine her response
to bloated and floating
salt-water corpses:
"Weh . . . sa maumau!"

Va

I spent my adolescence
in a town grown up
around sugar.

Walked the hour-less kilometers
to school through the dust
of cane

tall stalks of sweet grass
bands upon bands of
green, red, gold and green again
mapped our boundaries

hot days ballooned
with the smoke of cane burned
down to the soil
black and brittle

the scent of milled sugar
leaked into our dreams
on nights cool and cloying

school breaks
when the heat ripened mangos
and flash-dried the wash on the lines
my cousins and i sat on doorsteps

sweetness the stem of refrigerated dovu
in our hands

sweetness the tearing of coarse stalk
methodically with our teeth

sweetness the mouthfuls chewed dry
and spat into the communal pile before us

Lima

sugar is british colonial rule sugar is native lands stolen
by white settlers for plantations sugar is girmityas fed
lies who survived the long journey over oceans from
native to alien lands and enslavement sugar is the blood
of girmityas, itaukei and blackbirding slaves from vanuatu
and the solomons to fatten the pockets of settlers and
the native elite sugar is sacred dovu made toxic through
refinement and poisoning the vanua

Ono

Suka is to return

Degei Dakuwaqa Daucina
remember your lost children
forgive us our sins
deliver us

Suka is to return

Meke Vula

Galu (shhh . . .)

In the time of darkness
(they say) we worshipped
the moon   in the dark
days   the moon
bukete, her belly a basket
a sail in full wind
(they say) we danced
alone   for her

Galu (shhh . . .)

In the time of darkness
(they say), nights   black
skinned as the lips
of women tattooed
by dauveiqia
(they say) we danced
naked   before her
the moon

Galu (shhh . . .)

Some days (they say)
we
still
do

vaka tevoro (we call it)
devil ry

our kin
ancestors

spirits

vu

black   magic (they call it)
witchcraft

to spill kava for the vanua
to dance naked for the moon
to serve as medium
for ancestors

galu
silent
my tongue
broken in English

galu
mute
my knowledge
schooled in English

galu
dumb
my genealogy
mutilated in English

Galu (shhh . . .)

in the days dark
with ancestors
we kept time with the moon
by harvests waxing, waning
of yam, land crabs, nuqa
and the flowering

of doi trees . . .

Galu (shhh . . .)

some dark nights
in the light of the moon
I dream of merevesi
my bubu's mother
healer, herb-gatherer,
bone-setter
medicine maker
gifter of fertility

Galu (shhh . . .)

Some nights she wakes me
the moon
the light of her belly
pooling over the round of mine
dance, she laughs
au bolei iko

Some days
I do

Ai Domoniwai

all rivers begin
where lomālagi and qele
meet
mount tomanivei
the land's crest
nai ulu-ni-vanua
cleaving the heavens
for rain

all of us mudlings

ro etuate navakamocea mataitini
my great-grandfather
a river delta man
the vunivalu, warrior-chief
of lomanikoro
like his fathers before him
mangrove   men
growing heart and silt roots
a mudwater fortress
anchoring the vanua
nursing its lifeblood
with mana
moci, kai and bonu

here the people are via
giant mud taro
salt and fresh water
fattened

my bloodline weaves
through the rewa river veitiritiri
mudflats

like the bonu

        slippery   mangrove
        eel

        for eel

        to whet
        your appetite
        hunt with your hands
        make eyes of your fingertips
        in the kava slick mud
        between tiri and dogo
        reticulated water trees

        for eel

        to sate
        your hunger
        yield skin and blood
        to this mouth
        for i   am no duna
        i will not
        give up life
        to bear you fruit
        without your
        offering

        ai gusuniwai

        all flesh and fluid mouths
        feed
        where lomālagi and qele
        mate

all rivers   snake
rivulets in earth's flesh
to the ocean's arms.

Letter to my people (for Palestine)

to those of us
i-taukei
for whom 3 decades
of fijian
UN "peacekeeping"
in the middle east
has bought for israel
our eyes and mouths

once the world told florid tales
of our warriors' courage
war clubs carved from vesi

ivei na neimami yaloqaqa?
where is our spirit
now?

show me
the bravery
in speaking for
the powerful

show me
the courage
in looking away
from the tearing of people
from their vanua
children from mothers
farmers from orchards
fishermen from the deep sea

have we forgotten our own
removals
lost land, birthright

to british & native elite allegiances?
       i-taukei   sold, exiled
       indentured laborers
       on our own lands
       the vanua turned
       sugar teat to suckle settlers

       where has our spirit fled?
       in pieces
       with remittances
       western unioned from Sinai
       Lepanoni
       the Golan heights
       to morris hedstrom
       shopping centers
       in suva, nadi,
       navua, ba . . .

       where has our spirit fled?
       sacrificial burial
       beneath the yavu
       of homes   a nation
       bought with Israeli shekel
       and gaudy romances of lost tribes

       defiling the vanua
       disrupting our mana

       to those of us
       i-taukei
       for whom over 2000 palestinians dead
              over 500 of these   children
              in just
              one

summer
is justified

once, newly independent
of british colonialism,
our people rose
a forest of vesi
warriors for a nuclear-free pacific
against the combined forces of french,
american and british imperial powers.

once, we sang songs in solidarity
around kava bowls all night
with black south africa
against an apartheid regime

ivei na neimami yaloqaqa?
where is our spirit
now?

when israel kills
little boys gone to the beach to play
bombs hospitals bursting with wounded
shells schoolrooms sheltering the lands' orphans
erects apartheid walls between kin
forbids gaza's fishermen rights to their qoliqoli
uproots centuries-old Palestinian olive trees
by the thousands

ivei na neimami yaloqaqa?
where is our spirit
now?

once ratu sukuna dreamt of sovereignty

restored through battle
the people's spirit triumphant in a national military

but
before we were soldiers
we were fishermen
before we were soldiers
we were farmers
before we were soldiers
we were warriors of the vanua

ivei na neimami yaloqaqa?
where is our spirit
now?

No-Name Poem

Perhaps new words will form
New words will form, if I can shift—
The soil
Sand
Dirt
Beneath the current
Beneath my feet
At the root of my own tongue.
Perhaps, if I wiggle my toes, just so . . .

Perhaps I can imagine new letters
New letters
Like DNA strands
If my body churns out memories
Stories
Songs
To heat this ripple, these waves, this pool.
Perhaps, if I stir the water with the twisting of my torso, just so . . .

Perhaps if my rage were to fuel the strength of this undertow
Or my love calm this eddy
Like a lullaby
Old words will change their meanings.
Perhaps, if I swallow then spit out salt water,
Sweetened by my breath
Quickened by my heartbeat
Swirled over my tongue
Just so . . .

aue . . . oiaue . . .

Perhaps I will recover lost words

aue . . . oiaue . . .

Native Poem I

The Other Woman

all this Talk
of Colonizers and Colonized
Centers and Margins
Self and Other
does her no good

on the Margins
of the village
stand two churches
where men and women
are set apart

home-coming,
she is made dumb finally
by all this naming
of Oppressor and Oppressed
it mangles her tongue

in the village center
women dance and sing
in native
tongues.

on the periphery
she sits
mouthing
silent words.

Native Poem II

native
       tongues
       woman
home

native
       tongues
       home
woman

native
       woman
       tongues
home

woman
       tongues
       home
native

tongues
       woman
       native
home

tongues
       native
       woman
home

home
       tongues
       woman
native

Native Poem III

Yameyalewavanua (tonguewomanland)

yameyalewavanuayalewayamevanuayame
yalewayamevanuayamevanuayalewa
vanuayamevanuayalewayame
yalewayamevanuayalewa
vanuayameyalewa
vanuayalewa
vanuayame
yalewa
yame

yame
yalewa
vanuayame
vanuayalewa
vanuayameyalewa
yalewayamevanuayalewa
vanuayamevanuayalewayame
yalewayamevanuayamevanuayalewa
yameyalewavanuayalewayamevanuayame

yameyalewavanuayalewayamevanuayame
yalewayamevanuayamevanuayalewa
vanuayamevanuayalewayame
yalewayamevanuayalewa
vanuayameyalewa
vanuayalewa
vanuayame
yalewa
yame

yame
yalewa
vanuayame
vanuayalewa
vanuayameyalewa
yalewayamevanuayalewa
vanuayamevanuayalewayame
yalewayamevanuayamevanuayalewa
yameyalewavanuayalewayamevanuayame

lolomaloha: fruit for aiko

this pomelo is a poem   a canoe
fleshed of poetree   for distances
for sistering and brothering
i mean   kin-ship
for travel across this
our blue skin

this pomelo is
a setting off   star-shipping
with dried seeds, smoked fish
and fresh coconut   genealogies
to story ourselves   a/niu

this jabong is a   camakau
sunset pink   translated
your citrused
tongue to mine   friend-ship

steered by talanoa
wayfinding with   lolomaloha
na 'āina momona

Kokoda (for Tere)

Kokoda-making is a homecoming
to Sunday feasts on sweltering Fijian afternoons
miti-soaked bele
ika and dalo
with lemon, salt, and chili

Kokoda making is a homecoming
calls to mum and aunties across datelines
searching for names of fish
in mother tongue

In San Francisco
Una and I
lacking a machete or even a butcher knife
slam Safeway coconuts against concrete stair edges,
rush to capture the juice
before it runs into the street below
our laughter an equatorial sun

Kokoda making is an act of love;
cubing fish into mouthfuls
juicing fistfuls of lemon
coconut scraper straddled,
cupping white fruit to metal teeth
scenting the air
of earth
the lean of trees towards ocean
skin clothed in coconut oil

Kokoda making is resilience
In Waikiki where the niu is stripped of fruit
I use cans of Thai lolo
I have lost my scraper en route to Hawai'i,
and the one at Na Mea—decorated with shell inlay—is $90

not for everyday use.

Across from the Ala Moana
my family sits down to eat at one
and finishes near midnight
a feast of kokoda, sushi, mussels with lolo
curried pork and Nikola's fish soufflé.
We nourish ourselves with talanoa
between meal tides
stories of home
and savory gossip.

I promise myself
the next time I stop at the Fiji Market
in Kahuku for dal and roti
I will buy a new scraper.
One of these days
my kokoda will be as good as my mother's

Cawaki / sea urchin

careful hands
undress
      bare
your fleshed
heart
      splayed
in spine—
hollow
      star-fished

i take
your tongue
      oranged
on mine
sea
butter sweet
brine

stories she sung me/for katalaine

o o baua
lai vei iko tinamu
lai qoli keidaru

daru na mai tatavu
kemu na saku
qau na damu
o o baua
            traditional lullaby

some women are made
for mothering
not you

you would let the sky
cradle me
baptized
in the choice of my
own gods

you would let the sun
clothe me
oiled down in bubu's
reliable brown hands
mokosoi and coconut
fragrant

you would let the earth
feed me
mouthfuls of ripened pawpaw
softened dalo
and fish you'd chewed

later you taught me

to love curried crab

      so hot our skin sweat
      tiny licks of flame

      you would let the men
      name me
      my father choosing carefully
      with his year-old fijian tongue
          tagi
      while you called me
      pumpkin-pie
      your guji girl

      you would let the rain
      teach me lullabies
      of the land
      the humid air fill my lungs
      and song
      with loloma

      o o baua
      lai vei iko tinamu
      lai qoli keidaru

      daru mai tatavu
      kemu na saku
      qau na damu
      o o baua

secrets

i release
relinquish
these secrets
this one
and this one
about my mothers
about myself
i will peel the skin off this secret
spoon out its soft
insides
feed them
to you
this one i will crack open
like a coconut
under the blunt edge of a machete
i will pour out its juice
and bathe you in it
so you awaken
and I heal
i will re-seed
my center
fill my
insides
anew
with sweetness
grow new skin
soft and brown
i will retrieve
my soul from
sunlit
stained glass
temples
of childhood
and peace will leak

through my pores
        like sweat
        the scent of guava

Reguregu for JL

the day after
i learn
about you
on facebook

sweet boy
brilliant boy

the day after
i learn
about you
i am two years late
to your wake

this reguregu
a thin ibe woven
of memory
time worn
a poor farewell

where i would keen
the day after
i learn
about you
i feed the hollow an american
burua, death feast
egg mcmuffin
hashbrowns
mozzarella sticks
coffee

in lieu of communal
mourning, in this place of plastic
toys and happy

meals i sit alone
with macbook and wifi
connection
the distance between us
        4024 miles
        sixteen years
        so many canoes's breaths
        between the lands
        of the living and the dead
                privilege
        the distance between us

my screen weeps
stories of your death   alone
as only a 27-year old indian kid
can be   alone
in his own home lands
at 4am in january
nebraska winter

two years too late
i pray the land
warmed
to your body
a quilted blanket
two years too late
i pray it sang you umo^{n}ho^n
lullabies

so far from you and late
to your wake
i mark the time in nights
since your crossing
        paths with death

       in the shape of another
       poor man's
       blade
       death
       the shape
       of another
       black man's
       rage
you who survived
       death
       the shape
       of settler colonialism
you who survived
       death
       the shape
       of anti-indian and
       anti-black racism
you who survived
       death
       the shape
       of educational apartheid
       and police violence
it is a marvel you lived
at all

two days after
i learn about you
i weave my own stories
remembering

the nonprofit [industrial complex]

that paid me
indigenous pacific kid

CAN Americorps stipends
to "help" kids like you
black and indigenous
to these stolen plains
umoⁿhoⁿ

your 6th-grade classroom

tracked
special education
learning
your place
with patrick, and angel
josiah, and ashley
rick and shane and shelly
and hope, the indian
girl mrs brown
said was fine
          i did not
register
hope

afterschool programs

feeding you expired
foodbank snacks
your eyes as you read
their use-by date
wide and knowing
stipends gone
to fresh fruit and
activity books
filled
with lessons

that afternoon

i drove you home
last, just us in the dead
of winter
your face the sun
flickering
you   eleven
twice the age of my exile
for school so far from ocean

i struggle
to tell you
sun child
sweet child
your heart a pow-wow drum
in your little man chest
i struggle to weave you nets
the shape of safety
with the weight of my words
the flimsy of my wish
you are special
i say
through education you could
        escape
        [jump federal poverty thresholds]
        [trespass educational apartheid zones]
        [evade this police state]
it
gets
better

the day after

i learn
about you

núzhiⁿga qtáthewáthe
núzhinⁿga wéudaⁿ

i am two years late
to awaken
to your death
in peter pan park
where you'd played
native land
enmeshed, disciplined in
lincoln city grids
A to Z and numbered

i am two years late
to waken
to your passing
in peter pan park
halfway between
university of nebraska
campuses, the distances
between which i walked
while boarding

the day after
i learn
about you

núzhiⁿga qtáthewáthe
núzhinⁿga wéudaⁿ

the day after

i learn
about you
on facebook
two years late
to your wake
my search filter
resurrects you
victim

two years after
your death
so violent
the state sentences
your murderer 18 to 20
three quarters of your
life time
for manslaughter

two years
after your death
so violent
the state
in nebraska vs parker
argues the diminishment
of umo^{n}ho^n lands and
sovereignty

núzhi^{n}ga qtáthewáthe
núzhi^{n}ga wéuda^n

just hours after they learn
of your death
your family and friends
held vigil sung songs

a fire for your
winter night's flight

a few hours to
launch a petition
to light the park
a week to
organize a march
demanding justice
in your footsteps
#j4jl

núzhiⁿga qtáthewáthe
núzhiⁿga wéudaⁿ

two years too late
i pray the land
warmed
to your body
a quilted blanket
two years too late
i pray it sang you umoⁿhoⁿ
lullabies

PERMISSION TO MAKE DIGGING SOUNDS

Noʻu Revilla

bath water

When I was a baby girl I was bathed in the sink
chrome mountains rising around me faucet water
fall lukewarm gurgle of tap water & Jergens I had
a pond & up above in the sky of my mother's
chest a necklace gold pendant flash of fire quick
enough to catch the name HAUMEA my father's
name engraved in black passed down to him by his
grandmother who gave birth in a cave passed
on the backs of lizard women who bathe in poʻowai
HAUMEA shape shifter HAUMEA seaweed seeker
HAUMEA crab catcher kukui nut fists that protect
prosperous impenetrable pōhuehue hips wet with
Haakolea HAUMEA vanishing HAUMEA birthing
may I sit w/ you shape shifter drink w/ you wai
o Kapuna my kūpuna swam in the currents of
your voyage from Kahiki swam in the stomach of
this vast & dark moana opened their wombs I am moʻo
puna moʻo wahine obey rocks slime & wai wai
wai HAUMEA may I bathe w/ you my mind
is a pond you poʻowai cleansing these now bitter
waters these mountains this sky HAUMEA many
bodied many named I ask your permission.

Make Rice

I rinse fists of brown grain with
water that comes from the faucet and
even if I can't afford it, I take
the time to watch hard pellets
squeeze through my fingers
like hard brown children are squeezed
out of holes
in fences
on private property.
Pouring dirty water out,
shooting faucet water in.
But I never lose a piece of rice
because that could be my daughter.

Getting ready for work

some things specific:
    Lancôme powder foundation
    in a black case
    with a mirror.
    A row of pink tiles on the bathroom wall.
    Doorknobs.
    15 carpet stairs.

other things:
    that I worshipped my mother's lipstick,
ate her nylons, and read the Bible for her.
I remember only that Eve is more evil than
the serpent so she sews prayers into my dresses.
    I know what serpent means.

            Mother often
            Mother make up
            Mother do mother do

    that I never imagined her as creature.
only mascara, Christmas
family newsletter face.
    She had no mouth no mouth,

            "Your mother had no mouth
before she met me."
                  thing: shattered.

    that his feet were Old Testament down
those stairs. that black case died an oyster
and the row of pink tiles shit themselves.
    my mother continued.
    her poor doorknobs.
    that eyeliner is surgery.

that choices are made to keep pretty -

Mother do mother do

I: mouth
eat pretty like glass.
Kiss and reflect how a child mirrors her mother,
how a door separates them like a terrible thing,
and the pretty is in pieces all over the floor.

baby girl, an etymology

pronounced bā- bee, not bahr-bee. they pronounced me *girl* forever. matrilineal term of endearment originally passed from mother-to-daughter-mother-to-daughter until my mother, who spoke proper english. so the girl passed on from aunties-to-niece and one day rumors spread this *baby girl* may not have babies of her own. related: babez, honey girl, girly girl, tita. tight-lipped. first recorded use, second grade '98 from aunty a. who *baby girl*'d me for washing dishes. aunty o. who *baby girl*'d me for mopping the kitchen. uncle k. who *baby girl*'d me with the end of a mop. this usage is obsolete in some of her areas. yet the figurative sense persists. the figurative precious or the making of precious is borrowed from childhood. like aunties borrow a daughter out of a niece. borrowing baby powder to clean me up after proper english fails. she is real. she is related to you. pronounced bā-bee, not bahr-bee. she is as real as the aunties who protect her.

Cutting Flowers for the Dead

I hate walking in cemeteries. Born & raised respecting the dead, I try my best to obey the narrow pathways between tombstones and burial plots. "Sorry uncle," to the dead & commemorated man. "Sorry, aunty," to the dead & commemorated woman. *1986–1987 MY SWEET CHILD, WE ARE SO SORRY.* Damn. I try not to curse in cemeteries. Born & raised respecting the dead, I try my best but damn. Maybe if I kept my mouth still and let the curse erupt and finish in my throat. Maybe if I kept it in my stomach, growling. The dead forgive hunger. Or maybe, just maybe, I keep it way down, where my body buries things. Like uncle's falsetto voice - may he rest in peace. His fat lips. His drunk wife. Screen door, hairy chest. Carpet soaked in beer the sound of no one coming to stop him. Our backs on cold tables. Gutted. Like fish. I hate walking in cemeteries. There's no cutting across the dead.

Bilum, For Rosa

back and forth bilum carry baby yams and river water.
no government rice because bilum swallows her forehead,
shining brighter than hospital gowns, bilum march for morning star,
knowing on her back bilum bush knives potatoes and fifteen years in prison.

dim-dim afford store-bought string. long-legged, short-skirted
fashionista buy brand name only, baby, the best bilum not knowing
brand bilum bought on the backs of others "eco-ethical" in Paris
"eco-ethical" in Brisbane "eco-ethical" in Waikīkī but no ethics in
West Papua. killing them like mosquitoes since 1962.

rosa crossed the border bilum. carry vegetables and referendum.
they want to make her disappear bilum. they want to steal her bow and
arrow throat and machete the sky – that's what happens when Indonesia
owns the right to breathe. meri bilum break your peninsula forehead make
international waters of your hair while islands collect at your neck
bleed black and red bilum. petitions on fire. meri carry the weight of the world.

West Papua. Merdeka.

Grandma Was A Gambler

Her house was raided & she was taken from 871 Pōhai Street.
The woman who made my dad and 11 others at 871 Pōhai Street.

Maui County was officially bat-shit about gambling rings and drug lords.
Take her out of the chicken fight, but not the chicken fight out of Pōhai Street.

The only woman arrested, only woman named in the papers the next day.
No clue *napintas* emptied ashtrays each week, smiling on Pōhai Street.

Clean astrays, Ooka plastic bags, boiled peanuts for life.
The sliding glass door was a world away on Pōhai Street.

The smack of playing cards, every sticky *napintas, come, come here.*
Never leaving grandma's house empty-handed, never from Pōhai Street.

Cigar smoke wrapped the garage like gauze.
Napintas are open cuts on Pōhai Street.

Dorothy, after hours

To the girl holding the
faucet in her hands

like a wand, like a good
witch: I left my dress in the

sink for you after a
hard day's work, my

bra stuffed w/ sea
shells & prescriptions.

Boy, I could love
playing wife.

If I click my
heels & lick the

yellow brick road
out of you, could you

let the water run
& squirt way

too much dish soap,
blow bubbles up my

dress w/out rubber
gloves & call

me home? Call me like
there's no home like me

like dish soap in bulk

for all the blowers &

witches & nine-to-five
brides playing wet.

Boy, I could love
playing dress up

in the sink w/ other dirty
dishes. But to the girl

holding the faucet in her
hands: blow home.

A dress for a dress.

moon bottom

bottom: to be under, beneath, the deepest part

last night, hina brought a black box. don't blush. a box is a box
even when it's black. in the box last night were hina's black
straps. fortified banana leaves, she says.
do banana leaves depress the skin? leave light bruises on the pelvis?

bottom: the myth of submission

last night, hina brought a black box. don't rush. she came to me
hard as a reef. from the box she fished her double-stitched black-
ness, the tide in me rising & rising. around her thighs the straps
tattooed themselves, like a chant, like a safeword. hina entering,
not as a man, not as a god. the moon herself. her mouth bright &
steaming.

bottom: sinking

last night hina brought a black box tonight you'll return home
put mouth to pillow & ask if the box means sky if hina packs
a planet. don't. the sky is not a fetish. i will take the moon away
from you. i take the sky.

#aloha'āina goes to the doctor

Your symptoms, please.
Nausea.
Shortness of breath.
Law enforcement.

Describe the pain, please.
It starts in my summit.

Point to the exact location of the pain, please.
Where my rituals live.
Where my kissing patterns learn gods names learn altitude.
My summit, their science.
Sometimes I feel like 13,796 feet.
But sometimes I feel like choking.

Continue with your pain, please.
One point four billion dollars.

Continue with your pain, please.
Words don't work properly anymore.

> STATE: Protestors
> PEOPLE: Do you mean "protectors"?

> STATE: Ceded lands
> PEOPLE: Do you mean "seized"?

Please, seizing is normal.
And my lungs? Are my lungs arrested too?

Restrict yourself to the most frequently asked questions, please:
"Is there Wifi?" "Where are the restrooms?" "Are there shuttles?"
Without oxygen, I am just a Visitor Center.

Your pain, please.
Worship for the worse:
300 full-time construction jobs
120 permanent jobs.
For the visitors.
For the next visit.
For the next generation.

Your pain, please.
Will it always burn like this?

Your pain, please.
Give me back my altars.

Your pain, please.
Let me eat my rocks.

Your pain, please.
My name is Mauna a Wākea.

Point to the exact location of the pain, please.

[where are you pointing?]

selections from Dream City, Eat Sugar:
A Sequence on 1950s Kahului

I. PROLOGUE

In 1893, the Hawaiʻian Kingdom was illegally overthrown. Hawaiʻi remained a U.S. territory until statehood in 1959, when, in the daze of post-WWII glory, a new American dream was sweeping the nation. With a booming economy, the idea of owning a home was fast becoming the foundation of a new way of life in the country. Even in Hawaiʻi, plantation homes were evacuated and families seduced into residential subdivisions.

On the island of Maui, the old port town of Kahului became the darling of development and was affectionately nicknamed the Dream City. Together with the Kahului Development Company, Harland Bartholomew and Associates, a Missouri-based city planning team, developed a master plan for homes, businesses, schools, churches, and parks. On January 7, 1950, *The Maui News* devoted its entire front page to photographs of the first home open for viewing. The average price of a complete home was listed at $7,250, and the first houses were built on both sides of Puʻunēnē Avenue. From the 1950s to the 1980s, more than 3,200 families bought house-and-lot packages in 14 installments. At its peak, houses were being sold every two minutes.*

Kahului was alive, and its nickname was no accident. The words "Dream City" produced a sexy and haunted relationship between the material reality of Kahului as a city and the imagined space of home-ownership and modernity for Hawaiʻians on the brink of American citizenship.

---

* "Development coincided with closing of plantation housing." *The Maui News 1900–2000:100 Years As Maui's Newspaper*. Wailuku: Maui News, Print.

II. HOW TO FIND US

According to *Place Names of Hawai'i*,
>KAHULUI: Town, elementary school, port, bay, railroad,
>and surfing area known as Kahului Breakwater.

According to daughters born and raised,
>Kahului is located on the neck of Maui.
>Kahului is the neck of Maui.
>Kahului is necking Maui.
>Necking, the Dream City.

III. How to Make a City Out of Sticks

In 1893 carrier pigeons arrived at Kahului, Maui.
One was brought to Honolulu and released with a letter tied to its neck.
It flew back to Kahului.

Puunene Avenue will be a fine boulevard with 100-foot right-of-way and pavement of 36 to 44 feet. This width permits two girls walking home from school. This width permits two girls walking home from school never holding hands. **This width permits** two girls walking home from school never holding hands because they are holding brooms. Broom sticks broken in half.

All parts, sweep the streets.

A moving lane in each direction. One lane for parking on each side. "A bird died here," they tell each other. With a message on its neck. Thinking "sweep" not "scratch," "sweep" not "scratch." Sweeping, not scratching, all the way home. They were allowed to do something with **this width** except scratch each other. Both hands on the broom, they were told. Don't ask them what they did in school. Blow on their heads if they scratch in public.

All parts, sweep violently.

The main street will have two pavements, each 30 feet wide, with a medial strip to accommodate the rail tracks. Sweep or strip. Sit like your spine is tied to a broom. Walk home with your broom tied to your hands. "Look at *your* neck," they tell each other, brooms swinging in their strip areas. Aunties remember the feeling: the more you swept, the more they stripped you. Dirty streets amaze the broomstick. And what did you learn in school today? "You broom bitch," they tell each other.

All parts dream violently.

Bird feathers fly between their feet. They sweep them. "Into our hands?" they ask each other. They know better. **The two belt streets and one radial street will have a right-of-way 80 feet wide, a pavement 36 feet wide.** Because they are holding brooms and never holding hands,

[148]

the two girls walking home from school use the word "leash." Fresh bird feathers **will have the right-of-way.**

Part Violent

Two girls walking home from school decide to destroy the things on their necks. "Let's destroy them," they tell each other. Sometimes destroy means create. **Other streets will have a right-of-way.** Ask Aunties - **these dimensions compare favorably with good mainland standards.** "I'll do you if you do me," they tell each other. Destroy/ create. **This width permits ONE! this width permits TWO! this width permits THREE!**

Children at play.

IV. DADDY CANE

For every hard-working father ever employed at HC&S, especially mine

Was he a green, long sleeve jacket
& god-fearing man?
On the job, bloodshot.
Marrying metal in his heavy
gloves, bringing justice to his father,
who was also a smoking man.
No bathroom breaks, no helmets, no safe words.
He whistled sugarcane through his neck,
through his unventilated wife,
his chronic black ash daughters.
This is what a burn schedule looks like.
And if believing in god was a respiratory issue,
he was like his father.
Marrying metal to make a family.
At home he smoked before he slept.
In the corner with the door
ajar, cigarette poised like a first-born:
well-behaved, rehearsed.
Curtains drawn, bedrooms medicated.
He was always burning into something.
Part-dark, part-pupils.
For my father, the night was best alone.
When only he could see through
the world and forgive it.

V. HOW TO MICROWAVE DAUGHTERS

Please save these instructions for household use.
Do not stick your fingers inside
when the door is closed and the magic glass
table holding your daughters is turning,
turning, turning in place.
Please do not stick your fingers
inside your daughters
without giving them sticks
to slap away the heat and imagine consent.
To name her, assimilate her.
At least give your daughter sticks.
Please save this household.
When you stick them inside and the doors behind
your daughters slam shut, believe them.
They know how to close their mouths against exposure.
They know frozen in the center.
They bet their sticks on it.
Please save this house.
Through the heat your daughters
drag narrow-necked containers,
whispering about their powers
and rationing damp towels.
Their bright necks flashing enough to cook their insides.
Watch them through display windows.
Watch them turn into a house of sticks.

VI. GLASS, GRANDMA, AND GLUCOSE

In Dream City, there is a grandmother with a sliding glass door.
Come in, come in, she chirps. When her glass door opens,
there is light. But first, there were dirty sugar children.
Still, the plantation is shuttered, and she is modern now.

Look at her door. *Come in, come in,* she chirps.
She is taking glass in her own hands, like a cane cutter,
but she is no longer a plantation. She is shattering, shattering.
And over time, things go wrong, and homeowners prepare.

Because my grandmother's hands are glass, I am part shatter.
To open doors was to hold light hostage.
They forgot to call her homeowner.
In Dream City, there were women and smokestacks.

Fifty years later and light is still her hostage, locking
our days behind her chest so the cane in her burns.
When you see her, don't say grandmother. Say Dream City was
the real thing, say she was better than a smokestack, say
children always shatter like that, just like sugar.

protocol

kapa-beating night
hands are fatal, she is able
to destroy the night
does she capture you?

kapa-beating night
hands are fatal, she is able
to destroy the night
does she capture you?

kapa-beating night
hands are fatal, she is able
to destroy the night
does she capture you?

kapa-beating night
hands are fatal, she is able
to destroy the night
does she capture you?

kapa-beating night
hands are fatal, she is able
to destroy the night
does she capture you?

Memory is a reef.
Origins hiding, predators hiding
in holes as big as men.
Who is hiding their blood inside
me?
I am the daughter of fishermen.
Born part-bait, sent to sea.
Seduction before I grew legs.
I learned to shine, hook, &
survive.
The bite marks, I memorize.
There is no weeping in salt
water.
Who am I bleeding legacy for
when I am cut alive?
Legacy let me keep my skin
but kept my fish blood hostage.
I hemorrhage to remember.
Remember my fishing line
veins can gut an empire.
I am the daughter of fishermen.
I hemorrhage to remember.
As hooks remember the fish and
blood remembers the bait.

dirtiest grand

How to enter Aunty Val's house when
our tits are hanging out &
Our Fathers are inevitably our uncles
stink, plucking us like 'opihi
for before, for smiling,
for clinging like we belong.
We're the ones with the tramp stamps
smoking Menthols like a big girl,
the ones with the big good for
nothing mouth but at least she
can pack left-overs.
We're the ones with keawe trees in the dark,
left with our tits out,
hugging toilets,
quick rinsing in the sink,
the clink of after-hours jewelry
bringing prayers back and forth
on earth as it is in heaven.
Forgive us.
Forgive Aunty Patsy.
Forgive the god of Heineken &
the gods of piss corners & knowing
who got who without asking.
Are we the dirtiest grand
daughters come to hula uncle's tarp?
Bluest tarp in Hāna?
When the stink rises because
stink rises & never leaves,
Aunty Val peels us out of
bed like labels off beer,
sends us not into temptation
but the kitchen
where we hold our own hair back.
Clean panties & a clean stove.

Debutantes for breakfast
& we gently decide who
will chop onions today.

for high tide

Have you ever seen the ocean weep?
Drop her head in her lap & crash?
If the ocean can keep a straight face & pretend, are any of us safe?

Dear sister, to me you have always been the ocean.
Pouring from our mother's body, salt-
skinned & reef teeth, you swallowed her hospital
bed & was vast. I was your black
net sister, dream of rope that broke waiting for
you in tight dark braids, broken
by fish men and fathers. Black net

                high tide. Sister,

you became the calm before
his storm before his foaming un
buckled belt wrists lashed your
back thrown against the rocks of furniture.
I became a black net when knuckles started
throbbing, when mouths wanted
something squirming & unshelled.
Drowning became a love song to the sunken
ship our father was. But a childhood &
two babies later, you still inherit the color
black like a bloodline but this is not the darkness of
our ancestors, the sweet black belly that birthed our
people is not your black eye he's rearranged your body
parts. I become a black net when your skin is
too puckered, when your arms fly out for
mercy & emergency rooms are too
bright to identify your injuries.

Dear sister, I am writing because you have a daughter now
who comes home telling stories of black magic home telling
stories of running away Aunty Aunty Aunty daddy broke
the house again Aunty Aunty Aunty mommy asking god
again Aunty ask god for me too. Sister,
this is not a letter to god, sister, this is not a prayer to
our fathers who art heaven – the world's first glass
ceiling. You sleep & pray for divine intervention dear
god may this ceiling hold his fury his black
blood hands. Glass ceilings mean nothing but your
own shattering. No mirrors to reflect no choices
to reflect on. Since when is to stay or die a choice?

Sis, I'm going to break stars for you so there is
more than hospital glow more than jailbird songs singing
bail money means rent money broken stars instead of light
bills "and then there was" fiction your bed time
ammunition against a man who thinks he can walk on water –

sister you are the ocean.

And if the ocean can keep a straight face & pretend,
are any of us safe?

Give a Damn Girls

Devastate me, again. Drop my body
like a bomb from your state-
sanctioned breasts, that mother
shelf, holding Bibles, holding prayer
circles like target practice for the girl
who became a bomb instead of good-

for-something daughter. *Nothing good
will come of this*, she told me. God owns my body
and the Bible is no girl meets girl, girls
fall in love, girls get certified by the state
story. Didn't you hear Kim Davis doesn't separate prayer
from government like my mother

doesn't separate prayer from targets, my mother
aims higher, heaven high like any good
Catholic woman. Armed & ready to pray her
daughter through the sins of her body,
sins of females and fornication – this is a state
of emergency. Warning, warning: girls

gone to college, girls gone wild, girls
gone AWOL from rom-com altars. Mothers
are weaponizing holy water in a state
of panic, wailing, drowning. *Nothing*, they say, *good
will come* of your body becoming her body
coming out without the word of God, praying

in tongues – but this is worship that looks like me, prayer
that looks at me like a girl in love, not a girl
in crosshairs. I refuse to be a ticking body
for a nuclear family, where a good mother
gives a damn if there are thousands of good
daughters out there. Girls are bombs, may the state

forgive them. But to every fallen daughter: we are not state-
ments of war. We are not fallout or wasted prayers.
Tonight, I'm going home, going down, showing how good
girls worship. And when my mouth opens, this girl
will come home, we'll make family without the market of mother
hood, and detonate each other. Un-droppable, un-damnable bodies.

Tonight, I give my body to her as a statement
of faith in love, in the mother of all prayers,
in all the girls who give a good damn.

Ceremony

Ladies and gentlemen, are we are gathered here today to join together in unholy matrimony these freshwaters of Hawai'i to this state of Hawai'i?

Do you, state, take these waters from our lives, to have and to own from this day forward, for development and profits, in sickness and drought, to divert, privatize, and distribute 'til poetry, sustainable practices, and informed protest do you part?

And do you, freshwaters of Hawai'i, take this state, to be your deeply unfortunate husband? To permit his narrow mind and slippery fingers their illusions, as if he could actually contain you, as if his green-green pockets could hold your roaring body, as if he could "I do" you?

And he hasn't met your salt water cousins yet.

His people don't have a word for the place where fresh waters and salt waters meet, eat, and genealogize, so on your wedding night, as you're remembering the cold, dark mountains you come from, your cousins will be rising and rising to find you, and your deeply unfortunate husband will be taken out to sea.

Rope / Tongue

for all the mo'opuna who jumped Hāna Bay Bridge

Grandma was a lizard at our age. She walked first, the story goes, and learned to climb. Up the stiff metal pole. Up and over the hanging head. Up up up until she was up and it was down.

The lamppost I thought was a cervix to the sky, but no. Not female. It was part-pier. And so we were born and pissed everywhere. On the bridge on the cracked concrete floor on the steps running down to the tires in the ocean where we waited for others to jump. Young, territorial. Everywhere pissing.

There was rope that hung from one end of the pier to the other, rope hung like a tongue, the kind of tongue we wished to have in our little girl mouths: thick twisted tasting salt in broad daylight. Big Girl tongue. In the water we mounted it squeezed it between our legs like she said slyly reproductive.

Grandma jumped into the ocean with her legs spread, landed, and the water turned to foam. The rope was dry for thirteen days. One for every child that swam out of her.

And we dreamed of sex in tents on cliffs in the morning out of wedlock making eyes biting lips saying I want I will I do and meaning the fuck out of it. The fuck of it formed like vowels between our legs - not like other girls and their ABCs - we knew rope like A E I O U.

One child from her forehead. One from her tongue. Another rolled out from her sweet jump spot. Another after another after another from her mo'o toes. They climbed. Like her. Grandma. Lizard. At our age.

Biographical Notes

KISHA BORJA-QUICHOCHO-CALVO is a Chamoru writer, educator, activist, and mother from the village of Mangilao on the island of Guåhan, in the Mariana Islands. She is currently a PhD student in the Political Science graduate program (with a specialization in Indigenous Politics) at the University of Hawai'i at Mānoa. Kisha's creative, academic, and community work are inspired by her Chamoru culture and history, local politics, motherhood, and the love for her home(is)land.

DR. JAMAICA HEOLIMELEIKALANI OSORIO is a Kanaka Maoli wahine poet / activist / scholar born and raised in Pālolo Valley to parents Jonathan and Mary Osorio. Heoli earned her PhD in English (Hawai'ian literature) with the completion of her dissertation entitled: "(Re)membering 'Upena of Intimacies: A Kanaka Maoli Mo'olelo Beyond Queer Theory." Currently, Heoli is an Assistant Professor of Indigenous and Native Hawai'ian Politics at the University of Hawai'i at Mānoa. Heoli is a three-time national poetry champion, poetry mentor and a published author. She is a proud past Kaiāpuni student, Ford fellow, and a graduate of Kamehameha, Stanford (BA) and New York University (MA).

TAGI QOLOUVAKI is Fijian-Tongan through her mother's people in Fiji—resilient coastal and river delta people from Sawana, Vanua Balavu in the Lau Islands, and Lomanikoro, Rewa on Viti Levu—and German, Irish, English American through her father's people. She was born and raised in Fiji, which is her home, and has lived in Utah, Nebraska, and California on the continent; currently, she lives with her love in Hawai'i. Tagi's work as a poet began in her absence from home/land, and in family/home spaces carved out by queer, African American, and Indigenous North American women poets. Her poetry is the work of a queer, indigenous Pacific woman struggling to way-find herself to the places of her ancestors in body, spirit, language, and loloma. Her poetry has been published in *Mauri Ola: Contemporary Polynesian Poems in English*, *The Yellow Medicine Review*, VASU:

Pacific Women of Power, and *Ika Journal*. Her art has been exhibited in *Diasporadic 679* in Otahuhu, South Auckland, Aotearoa/New Zealand, and *Down on the Sidewalk in Waikiki* in Hawai'i. She is grateful to her bubu, Ro Litiana Qolouvaki Mataitini, and her mother, Katalaine Vaiagina Rakai, for everything.

NOʻU REVILLA is a queer Indigenous poet and educator of Hawaiʻian and Tahitian descent. Born and raised on the island of Maui, she has performed throughout Hawaiʻi as well as in Canada, Papua New Guinea, and at the United Nations. Her work has been published in *Literary Hub, Poetry, Black Renaissance Noire, The Missing Slate,* and Poem of the Week by Kore Press. Her chapbook *Say Throne* was published by Tinfish Press in 2011. In 2012, the Honolulu Museum of Art featured her poetry installation *Altering Papers*, inspired by archival aloha ʻāina letters by Queen Liliʻuokalani. She also served as the Poetry Editor of *Hawaiʻi Review* (2013-2015) and organized the first Aloha ʻĀina Zine Workshop in solidarity with the protectors of Mauna Kea in July 2015. In 2017, she coordinated flash mob readings of Liliʻuokalani's letter of protest to the Provisional Government, one of which featured at the Women's March at the Hawaiʻi State Capitol. She is currently finishing her Ph.D. in creative writing at the University of Hawaiʻi-Mānoa.